THE PREMISE

J. Andrew Mosley

ISBN 978-1-0980-9402-7 (paperback)
ISBN 978-1-0980-9403-4 (digital)

Christian Faith Publishing
832 Park Avenue
Meadville, PA 16335
www.christianfaithpublishing.com

Printed in the United States of America

NOTE FROM THE AUTHOR

I loved baseball while growing up but was absolutely terrible playing it. I was weak and had an enlarged heart condition that took my breath away and crippled me with severe chest pains. Nevertheless, I wanted to play anyway. The coach of my church-sponsored team let me play either because "the love of Christ" constrained him to do so or because he just felt sorry for me. My teammates, of course, hated me. I couldn't play. And by the way, we nearly always lost pitifully to most of the teams we played with, especially to a team named the Hill Top Junior Dukes.

All was not lost. An occasional ray of hope would penetrate our gloom because we won when the opposition didn't show up. I learned the meaning of the word *forfeit* early in my life. The Dukes and other teams regularly refused to grant us the dignity of playing them so that they could beat the living daylights out of us. Man! They were good at it!

The team I belonged to was called the Sharon Adventists. Why? Well, because we were from the Sharon Adventist Church—tah dahhh! Allow me to let you in on a little secret. Inwardly, I wanted to be a Duke! That sounded so much better, so way cooler. When you're young like that, labels make a huge difference.

I was assigned to right field—the safest place you can put your weakest player. Statistically, most baseballs course toward left field or center field because of the preponderance of right-handed hitters. There was another problem. I didn't own a glove. My big handicap was that I was left-handed and needed a glove that fit my right hand. There weren't any available, so I had to play barehanded.

I was ridiculed and laughed at by both my teammates and the opposing team players on most game days. I couldn't field the ball because it hurt to trap it with my bare hands. I couldn't catch pop flies because they hurt my fingers when I tried to intercept them. So there I stood—so black, so poor, so timid, so afraid, so without a glove to protect my bony hands, and so without acceptance to protect my bony heart, marooned in the middle of the grassy right-field desert, hoping by the *grace* of God that nothing came my way ever! On most game days, that prayer seemed to be answered. But one day, another answer came, or maybe it was a question I had to answer.

Wooooosssshhhhh! went that bat. Then—*thraaaacccckkk!* A Duke hit a high-arching pop fly that was headed—not middle, not left, but right and up at first and then down speeding toward me. Me of all people! You've got to be kidding me! It was going to hurt! I stood there trembling with both my mouth and eyes frozen wide open. A supernova could not have hidden the glare coming from my peepers and pearly whites as that ball descended toward me. The whole field went silent. It seemed like the whole world listened for the drop of that pin, that ball, because they knew it would soon land by my feet with me standing and stunned right there—stunned, embarrassed, trembling, and bewildered as usual. It was the final play of the game, and you guessed it, there was no chance for the Sharon Adventist to win. The Dukes, as usual, had walloped us. But here came that ball faster and faster.

And then, it happened. I remembered what my mother taught me. In desperation, I closed my eyes, stretched my open fingers toward the heavens with the heels of my palms tightly held together, and prayed, "Dear Jesus, help me to catch the ball!" I didn't say, "Amen." I didn't need to because I suddenly felt the ball fall snugly into my outstretched hands making a "chupe-clutch" sound! I didn't move, and it didn't hurt! Did I hear cheers from my teammates? No. Were there any groans from the Hilltop Junior Dukes? Nope! Nada! I opened one eye, then the other, and couldn't believe what I saw. My teammates were frozen in disbelief at what they saw! *The Dukes couldn't believe it either!* There was only a field full of pearly whites and peepers everywhere!

As I walked in from the outfield, I declared with innocent joy to everyone, teammates and others, that, "Jesus helped me catch the ball!" That declaration, however, was met with considerable scorn and ridicule, especially from my so-called "fellow church member" teammates. For a long time afterward, they teased me mercilessly about my singular accomplishment, *"Jesus helped me catch the ball,"* mocking my voice inflection and hand gestures while doing it.

It stung. Yes, it stung a lot. But the hope and faith born in me that day has encouraged me to reach for the stars for all the things that many discouragers in my past have said was beyond me, unattainable, not expected, and too far beyond my poor power to add or detract! "Amen," said they of their denunciations. No matter. He who sits high in the heavens had other plans for me.

Now do I catch every ball? No. I've learned that I don't need to. And it's all right because I've caught enough of them by the *grace* of God in my sixty-seven years that I have more than a few to toss back and forth with others.

Hey, let's play catch.

No worries.

One rule

Glove provided—none required!

ACKNOWLEDGMENT

I am indebted to my mother who died of complications of congestive heart failure and liver cancer in 2006, on my birthday. Amid the chaos, trauma, and confusion of my childhood, she was an island of hope, patience, perseverance, and love.

When I was in junior high school, bullies were abundant, and I was often one of their favorite victims. One day after PE class, I went to my locker after showering to get dressed and was horrified to realize that my school clothes were missing. I called my mother at home and told her what happened. It wasn't that I hated telling her. It's just that I knew Momma didn't have the car because my father drove it to work and my school was eighteen blocks away from our house.

After I told her what had happened, the only thing she said was, "Don't worry, son. I'm coming." Momma was overweight, overworked, and burdened down with many things. And now, she had to somehow bring clothes to the number 3 child of her seven. How?

Then as I began to leave the locker room to go outside and wait for her, I spotted my missing clothes in a corner on the floor. So relieved, I hurriedly dressed and called home to tell Momma the good news. But she had already left? How? Was she walking? There weren't any buses running that often in the middle of the day back then. I worried.

Momma was overweight. She was chubby and round my entire lifetime. I was afraid for her. I knew she had worked all day cleaning a Jewish lady's house in the nicer area of town and that she was tired. She had been home cleaning our house and preparing dinner, and at the same time, she had to get ready to go to her three to eleven in the afternoon nurse aid job at the hospital where I was born. I stood on the loading dock at the back of the school, staring up the street into the distance, wondering when and how she would come. A long time passed. Then I saw something.

A lone figure way up the street slowly rocked from side to side coming toward me. There seemed to be no hurry. Progress was steady, persistent, and determined. No! I couldn't believe what I saw. Momma was on a bicycle. A bicycle? Really? I had never seen her ride a bicycle before, and I was happy and sad. I knew she had ridden all that way to bring me something that I didn't need anymore.

Momma rode up to me and stopped. If hope, patience, and perseverance could combine into one human face, Momma radiated them all. I apologized profusely for her having to come so far. I sighed. But she just said, "It's okay, baby. I'm glad you found them."

We chatted for a moment, and then, she turned around and slowly swayed away into the distance. I stood motionless watching her go—steady, persistent, and determined until she was too small to be seen anymore. Then I stood a while longer just looking in her direction.

Momma didn't leave me physical clothes to put on that day. She did, however, leave fresh clean clothes for my heart. I knew clearly that day what hope, patience, perseverance, and love look like, sound like, and act like. This book emerged, in large part, from what she brought patiently, swaying side to side, for me.

INTRODUCTION

For more than two hundred years, a fourteen-word sentence has been the foundation of America's self-declared right to become a sovereign nation. We can thank Thomas Jefferson and the Founding Fathers for this. When drafting the Declaration of Independence, Mr. Jefferson prefaced "the reasons for the separation" of the colonies from Great Britain with the words, *"We hold these truths to be self-evident, that all men are created equal."*

I believe Jefferson and the founders unwittingly infused this idea, this premise, with a brand of assumed righteousness of its own that has endured, unchallenged from their day until now. However, the more I thought about it, the more it puzzled me. Here's why.

Nearly everything I see around me in American society, not to mention other societies around the world, demonstrates just the opposite of this premise. I have read history of civilization and American history textbooks looking for self-evidence of created equality very closely. And perhaps most importantly, I have been alive on the earth for sixty-seven years; while during thirty of those years, I worked as a classroom teacher and school principal. That work required that I know what I know, find out what I don't know, and teach my students to know by questioning and to question what they think they know. This book practices that preaching.

"We hold these truths to be self-evident, that all men are created equal."

Consistent with the idea of life, liberty, and the pursuit of happiness for all, Jefferson's initial draft of the Declaration clearly denounced slavery. However, he opted to omit that language due to pushback from slave-owning founders, among whom he was included.

There were people during Jefferson's day who objected to the wording of the premise because it seemed hypocritical to leave it in the form shown above while depriving their slaves of its benefits. In spite of this, it seems to me that in the end, the wording shown above was left in place as a stand-alone abstraction, a wish with a ring to it masquerading as a profound principle. And that's the very problem I have with it. The premise has aged into a state of assumed unchallenged legitimacy.

This book is not another "Shame on you, America, for slavery" indictment. History is undeniable. Either face it or hide from it. It's your call. The point of this book is to think through Jefferson's premise and to explore ways to make American democracy more honest and secure.

"All men are created equal."

In *Hamlet*, Act 3, Scene 1, William Shakespeare wrote, "Conscience doth make cowards of us all." Unfortunately, too often, conscience is shunned, contradicted, and dismissed because its indictments are uncomfortable and inconvenient. For many, when personal gain is at stake, it is much easier to ignore the claims of conscience rather than embrace its implications and the possibility of healing the deep divisive wounds it reveals.

Conscience is a sharp stinging ointment when applied to raw intentions, plans, and deeds. Nevertheless, it is essential for binding up the wounds of any nation. Without it, wounds between people and nations remain wide open and fester to the point where each person dying away from the other becomes the default outcome of us all. However, this is not necessary. Truest bravery rescues the conscience from the cowardice of self. Truest bravery, in partnership with the conscience, has the potential to ultimately make not cowards but heroes of us all.

"We hold these truths to be self-evident…"

I ask that as you read this book, approach it like a painting that challenges you to discover its meaning for yourself. Feel free to pursue ideas that interest you well beyond the edges of the page. Words are keys, and ideas are passports. You may find some within these pages that grant you access to other keys and other ideas of your own.

CHAPTER 1

"We Hold These Truths"

To understand the phrase, "We hold these truths," one must determine just what truth is. Is truth based solely on absolute observable facts? (Is any observation absolute observation?) Or is truth relative and situational? Is there a one-size-fits-all common denominator called "truth" that is the reference space where all thoughts, actions, and facts of existence are compared and valuated before being embraced or debunked? If it is, how do we reach the point where we yield to its power to parse words, deeds, and perceptions in order to lay bare what was really said, what was really meant, the real reason why such and such a thing happened, and most importantly, how the world actually is? Is there a real "real"? Is an absolute "there" actually there?

Now Jefferson did not say, "We hold the *truth* to be." No, he said, "We hold *these truths*..." More importantly, Jefferson did not say, "*The truth is*," because to do so would have opened up a Pandora's box of argument about "Just what is truth?" Even Pontius Pilate's prisoner, Jesus of Nazareth, did not respond directly to that question. Or was it that Pilate didn't wait long enough for the answer? It could be that Pilate

intuitively knew the answer, was deeply troubled by its implications, and didn't dwell on it any length of time, choosing
rather to wash his hands of the effort rather than stare it in
the face and acknowledge its veracity. It's funny. People often
don't wait for the truth even when they ask for it.

When drafting the Declaration of Independence, I don't
believe Jefferson had any thought of provoking debate over
the question of what truth is. In the absence of a universal
reference point, the so-called truth is cliché. As long as cliché
goes unquestioned and can evoke distain against those who
question it, it will only be a placeholder of affected meaning,
a usurper, an interloper.

Meaning develops into deeply held truth in a variety
of ways. For instance, a loving mother tells her small child
not to touch the hot oven door because it can burn her. The
child listens to her words, but for some reason that may go
to the very core of learning about what truth is, she touches
the hot stove anyway, burns her hand, bursts into tears, and
runs to her mother. Why did the mother's dutiful warning
prove insufficient to prevent this event? I use the word *event*
here because it was no accident that the child reached out
and touched the hot stove anyway. She made a choice. Now
that her hand has a painful burn, the fact that a hot stove will
burn her is forever etched deeply into her emergent realization of truths. Truth seems to be able to pain and please and,
at times, do neither.

Perception is an essential ingredient in truth finding.
Our perception of truth is based on what we are able to know
and understand on a rational level. And what we are able to
know and understand is based largely on what we are able to
see, hear, feel, taste, smell, and reflect upon.

For those who embrace religion, truth is perhaps more
discernible on a spiritual level. Just what that means varies

from person to person. Belief in God, prayer, and adherence to biblical principles and doctrine seems to answer the need for establishing truth in their lives. Given this, it is interesting to note that the Christian Bible and the holy books and writings of most religions do not claim that their truths are self-evident.

Jefferson could have said, *"We hold by faith that all men are created equal."*

If he said that, the burden of proof would have fallen on him and his fellow patriots to give a reason for their so-called faith, either on the basis of a body of religious ideas or a secular philosophy that most readily underpins their position. Religious persuasions build up a body of beliefs, practices, and assumptions that are cemented together by repeated practice and adherence into faith positions that are uniquely held by them.

"We hold these truths..."

Consider a tree that falls in a forest with no one around to hear it. Does it make a sound? Is the answer a resounding yes because the impact of the falling tree against the ground *can* produce a series of compression waves in the atmosphere that *can* be interpreted as sound? The fact that there is no one around to interpret those waves as sound does not negate the fact *that they can be interpreted as sound*, depending on whether or not you are defining sound as those compression waves alone or the effect those waves have on the human auditory system. Therefore, because the tree *can* make a sound, it *does*; or does it?

Since there is no place on the surface of the earth where trees grow apart from the atmosphere surrounding it, sound waves *must* be generated if a tree falls to the ground. Or should we say a disturbance wave occurs? Are the waves themselves *sound*? Or is the interpretation of the disturbance they cause in the atmosphere *sound*? You want me to take a position, don't you?

Well, the sound is there because the compression waves and the sound response they generate in humans are part of an inseparable cause-and-effect relationship. We can judge the tree hitting the ground as producing a sound, even if we are not there to hear it, because we can easily extrapolate the experience of hearing it from our past experience of hearing that sound in person. That, my friend, is self-evident because the evidence is within oneself to reference a past experience and reach a conclusion that has maximum probability of being correct, given the new situation where one of the elements (being present for the actual falling of the tree) is missing.

Given the limits of human perception, we completely lack the ability to *know* atmospheric compression waves in any other way than what our brains interpret them to be. We can never know the truth of what sound actually is. We can only experience our contextualized mental construct of them. Evidently, that has been enough for us to get along in our neck of the physical universe and interact with it via a mental construct of the forms of energy that impinge on our senses. Need proof?

"We hold these truths..."

Go to sleep and dream. What are you seeing? What are you hearing? What are you feeling? Your eyes are shut. There are no sound waves going into your ears that correspond with the words or sounds you are experiencing in your dreamscape. There is no actual gravity holding you down or actual ground under your feet to orient you to which way is up or down. All things that you see, feel, touch, taste, and do in your dream are projected constructs of blended and reorganized nerve impulses (memories) that your brain generates in layers that when taken as a whole have become a living picture, a world, an illusion, a matrix loading program where you "think" you feel yourself being there. Nothing you experience in a dream is true. And for that matter, how much of what you experience in your so-called waking reality is actually true?

So if the tree is cut down right before your very eyes, falls to the earth while you are awake, and you don't hear a sound, can you conclude that it didn't make a sound? Or is it deafness? Or is it a lack of air as a conducting medium? In that case, I hope you're wearing a space suit. If a hearing person is standing right next to you when this happens, her perception is that it made a sound. Just because you didn't hear it doesn't mean that sound wasn't there. Limits to perception and interpretation do not nullify or debunk the existence of that which lies beyond such perceptions for whatever reason.

The human brain can only qualify and inwardly project representations of the various stimuli it receives. Our experience of reality is the mentally generated illusion of being immersed in a four-dimensional spatial-sensory place that includes time. Since matter is ultimately transformable to one form of energy or another, if we were able to "see" and experience the reality of our existence in terms of that energy alone, we could actually "know" what existence actually is. But we can't for now. Therefore, we must be content with the "reality theater" that plays out in our minds. Truth is an actor in part on the stage of that theater.

Jefferson said, "We hold these truths..." When did the Founding Fathers "touch the hot stove" and learn the veracity of the fourteen words, "We hold these truths to be self-evident; that all men are created equal"? Either this statement is true, or Jefferson just made it up for effect. Perhaps he listened to the mother of his own idealism, accepted her words on faith, and stepped out on the far end of an unsteady limb.

As a result of Jefferson's wording of his premise, a skir-mish line was established between what was embraced as truth by the emerging nation and what was embraced as truth by the British. Then, as there was no earthly arbiter of sufficient standing to rule on the merits of the truths held by each side, Jefferson wrote near the end of the Declaration the words, "appealing to the Supreme Judge of the world for the rectitude of our intentions."

Capitalizing the words "Supreme Judge" suggests that Jefferson was referring to God. Each side held generally sim-ilar views and beliefs about God. However, they each had opposing ideas about whose side the Supreme Judge would come down on. The emerging nation did not wait for a rul-ing from on high, and I suspect the founders only meant those words in a philosophical sense. It is like the saying, "Let the gods decide," which was popular in the days of ancient Rome. The problem with saying "We hold these truths" coupled with "appealing to the Supreme Judge of the world for the rectitude of our intentions" was that the effort on Jefferson's part to evoke the *Divine* in favor of his side was at best self-serving. Do these words cause the religiously sen-sitive to wince with discomfort? Perhaps they do. Consider this: Two Christian armies meet for battle in an open field. Before the hostilities begin, each commander prays for vic-tory over the other. Then the fighting begins and rages all day. Late in the evening, when the fighting stops, it becomes self-evident that one army has suffered far more casualties than the other. The losers subsequently retire from the bat-tlefield in retreat.

Now is it accurate to say that God favored one army over the other? Each army believed in him and prayed to him. Each army held to their own version of truths that sus-tained them in the battle. Yet one army lost. Could it be that the best answer to this question is that God didn't take sides in the battle? The same Bible that says that God is no respecter of persons certainly can imply that he is no respecter of armies. You see, when one or the other side deems his or her side to be right and the other wrong, an assumption is made that God sees it that way, too, and will prevail one over the other.

It is a mistake to legitimize a personal position by laying claim to divine favor without actually knowing if that selective favor exits. Perhaps, if the two sides had spent extended time trying to ascertain whether that favor with God existed for their position, the battle may have never taken place between them because, in the effort for each of them to be in favor with God, they would have found ultimately themselves in favor with each other. We know, however, that this does not happen in reality. Or can it?

"We hold these truths…"

I remember many years ago listening regularly to the *CBS Evening News* with Walter Cronkite. At the end of each broadcast Mr. Cronkite would sign off with the words, "And that's the way it is. This is Walter Cronkite, *CBS Evening News*, good night." He signed off this way each evening from April 16, 1962, until March 6, 1981, a span of nearly twenty years! I watched his broadcast from when I was nine years old until I was twenty-eight And what is remarkable about this is that during the entire span of his more than 2,500 broadcasts, I never remember anyone ever challenging the words, "And that's the way it is."

How can someone be front and center on television sets in living rooms across the entire nation over a span of nearly twenty years and say every night at the end of his broadcast, "And that's the way it is," and never be confronted about such an absolute assertion? The answer to this question may be that those who listened to Mr. Cronkite came to actually believe that things *were* just as he said they were. In fact, during his run as CBS news anchor, Mr. Cronkite gained the reputation of being the most trusted man in America.

So perhaps here, a lesson can be learned about truth and truths, given Mr. Cronkite's legacy. Truth in its rawest form may be taken to be "the way it is," regardless of how pretty and pleasant, distasteful and horrible, comforting or frightening, believable or unbelievable. When a news anchor of the standing of Cronkite said, "And that's the way it is," the people believed him, whether it was actually true or not.

Could it be that Mr. Jefferson saying "We hold these truths" possibly implied "Now you, British, this is the way it is"? So again, is truth the way something actually "is," or is it the way something is believed to be because a person of sufficient standing said it was?

"We hold these truths…"

I believe that the truth is "out there" and that it is knowable to the extent that our minds can understand and mentally construct a useful representation of it. I am also convinced that Jefferson's choice of the words, "We hold these truths," was used for effect to set a tone in a document calculated to achieve a desired outcome. And what an outcome it was—the establishment of a nation.

"We hold these truths…" "We hold these truths…" "We hold these truths…"

CHAPTER 2

"Self-Evident"

By definition, "something not needing to be demonstrated or explained" is *self-evident*. Self-evidence is also tacit because it is understood or implied without being stated. The actuality of what is called self-evident may or may not exist.

Let's begin this discussion with your very own right hand. Hold it up in front of your face. Is it self-evident that it is there? I believe that it is self-evident that your hand is there because it is attached to your body, you feel it, and you have control over where you position it in front of you. Besides, you can verify that it is there by using your left hand to feel it or by moving it closer and closer to your face until it makes contact with you. Or can you?

An understanding of the material world emerges from how our brains interpret sensory messages through the nervous system. Our brains are wired for *proprioception* or "the ability to know where our body parts are in space." If you suddenly lose your right hand in an accident, the corresponding center in the brain that informs you of where your hand is does not necessary cease to function. Often people who lose a hand can still "feel" it. They often feel their fingers and seem to know where their hand is, even though it isn't there anymore. Now, if you can neither see the hand nor feel it, is it there? What if someone tells you it's there? Do you believe them? Well, that seems more "other-evident" than self-evident.

If an individual declares something to be self-evident to onlookers that claim otherwise, he or she might be thought of as being unbalanced. For instance, a person says it is self-evident that there is a bird sitting on the fence post over there. If others standing with her do not see the bird sitting on the fence post, they may quickly conclude that she is imagining that it is there. If she continues to insist that it is there, they may decide that something is wrong because they cannot concur, at least visually, with what she claims to see. Conversely, if a group of people say to a lone individual that there is a bird sitting on the fence post and the individual denies it, the group can say that individual is either blind or crazy because she is unable or unwilling to concur with the group position.

It seems therefore that the esteemed actuality of any claim to self-evidence can be strengthened by concurring observations or claims. However, depending on the circumstances, the veracity of the group position could still be called into question. Yet this logic cannot stand on its own because self-evidence must be intrinsically realized, without the need to propping up by others. Right?

Finally, there could be two apparently credible groups who believe the opposite of each other regarding whether the bird is actually sitting on the fence. In this situation, each group could denounce other's position and escalate their hostility against the other to the point of open warfare. The late president Abraham Lincoln might say, "The intransigence of each excels the other."

After Jefferson stated that it is self-evident that all men are created equal, he did not offer any evidence to support his assertion. Instead, he mentioned certain inalienable rights—rights that the British crown did not recognize, and then, he offered examples of how Britain had violated those same unrecognized rights. I can imagine King George laughing with incredulous scorn at the idea.

I believe that Jefferson would have served the emergent nation and the cause of humanity in general more effectively if he had driven home his premise of created equality through a justification of the self-evident label he attached to it. He could have followed up the sentence "All men are created equal" with "This is self-evident because…" and then presented selected examples that could so positively support his premise that only deliberate close-minded refusal to hear or read the examples would result in their rejection.

Even though the definition of the expression *self-evident* is "not needing to be demonstrated or explained," in order to substantiate that very condition, a fact or situation has to have been previously known, seen, pointed out, discussed, and explained to the extent that common knowledge of it allows it to go without saying. Did any such common knowledge about equal creation of all men exist in Jefferson's day? What about from his day to ours today? Have we, as a nation, all known, readily seen, pointed out, discussed, and explained the created equality of all people among us until the idea has become common enough to call it self-evident? I don't think so. All of the evidence that I see confirms just the opposite.

"We hold these truths to be self-evident…"

I believe most people would be very hard-pressed to defend those words, even though they are sincerely believed while the logic that sustains them is uncertain. Many assent to the premise and pretend that it is true. It is taken for granted like a familiar speed bump that one gets so used to running over while driving the same way day after day. Normally, speed bumps are placed where a driver needs to be warned to slow down while approaching an intersection or where a road or highway ends. The premise is like a speed bump without an intersection to warn you away from.

When I heard the "I Have a Dream" speech by Dr. Martin Luther King Jr. for the first time, I was deeply moved. His voice resonated with the words, "We hold these truths to be self-evident, that all men are created equal."

Dr. King chose to use those words. Notwithstanding the cheers and applause that resulted, the insertion of the premise into his speech at that point was a speed bump, a punctuator, a Cronkite moment, where Dr. King had the floor or, should I say, the National Mall, where all his listeners were eager to hear and wanted to believe everything he said. I have absolutely no issue at all with that. There are times when logic and analysis are sidelined so that the need to believe may take the field.

Civil rights movement, with its desegregation case victories, did not advance any notion of created equality. The outward behavior of people was forced to change. Inwardly, however, racial disaffection, animosities, and aversions have continued to smolder. Those smoldering embers flare up severely from time to time into open violence and loss of life amid cries of "Blood and soil!"—cars running deliberately upon sidewalks to mow down peaceful protesters and the blazing hail of AR-15 bullets fired at children crouching for their lives under the desks they would otherwise be safely sitting in while learning how to read at school. As a result, we have now added "Principles of Hiding from an Active

Shooter 101" to the elementary, middle school, and high school curriculum.

"We hold these truths to be self-evident…"

If the premise had been a wish, a goal, a purpose to be actualized, the founders would have had something to work toward. However, the way the premise was stated implied that it was already a "there" that was there. What's more, Jefferson said *"created* equal," which necessarily implies that God made it so. Or was it more simply an idea he and others spawned—a verbal flourish, a garnish, an indigestible plate decoration? Certainly, Jefferson and the founders were not in the creating-of-equal-men business at the time. Who was? Who is today?

I believe Jefferson left the sentence about self-evident equality just as he wrote it because it evoked a literary effect. When it came to defending or explaining it himself, he was too morally compromised to venture upon any such effort. Oops! There was the matter of his ownership of slaves. I further contend that the vast majority of Americans who embrace the premise today are equally at an equal loss to explain or defend it.

The "reasons for the separation" indicated in the Declaration did not expand on the idea of created equality. The facts that Jefferson used to make his case were examples of British interference and the hampering of colonial life, liberty, and pursuit of happiness.

There were many reasons for the colonies to throw off British control—such as taxation without representation, the quartering of troops, confiscation of colonial property, and many other excesses and abuses Jefferson so eloquently pointed out as "the reasons for the separation." He complained that the actions of the British were meant to "reduce the colonies under absolute despotism." Jefferson made a very strong case while, at the same time, the American slavery system continued to capture, transport, and reduce men and women from the continent of Africa under absolute slavery. Which is the worse situation: Jefferson saying the British were deliberately trying to reduce the colonies under absolute despotism? Or the profit-driven practice of enslaving Africans, who were themselves actually reduced under slavery, a severe, inhumane, egregious despotism?

"We hold these truths to be self-evident..."

Now Jefferson could have written, *"We hold the obvious truth that all men are created equal."*

Wording the idea in this way would have left little to chance. It is straightforward and deliberate. However, such a statement would invite debate and objection, with the principal question being, "What is obvious about it?" I ask you the same question. Take a moment and think about it. Does anything pop into your head?

Did Jefferson and the founders know something in their day that we don't know in ours? What "hot stove" did Jefferson and his contemporaries touch to first learn this? I'll begin unpacking the expression "self-evident" by considering a circle.

CHAPTER 3

Self-Evident, More or Less

If I say that it is self-evident that a wheel is round, what is this self-evidence based on? Well, in childhood, most of us were taught that certain shapes have certain names. For example, your teacher may have held up a poster with the following shape on it and said, "This is a circle."

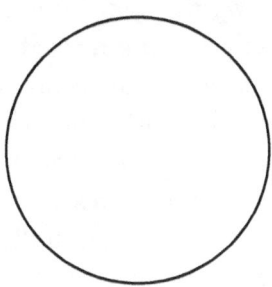

From that time forward, when this shape was presented to you, the word *circle* came to mind. If someone had asked you, "Why is this thing a circle?" you may have been hard-pressed as a kindergartener to offer any answer other than "My teacher told me it was."

Now as we grew up, we learned that a circle has a center and a constant radius or distance from its center to its curving line. We learned that the radius is constant all the way around the circle. Then we may have been given rulers to verify this, thus solidifying the concept in our minds. So now in addition to our belief in the words of the kindergarten teacher, in time we learned about measurements associated with the word *circle*.

Can I now hold it to be self-evident that a circle is round? Well, if I rely on the definition of *self-evident* as "something not needing to be demonstrated or explained," the roundness of a circle is self-evident to a person who is familiar with it, but it is not self-evident to someone who knows nothing about it or doesn't understand the language I am using to ask the question. In other words, self-evidence seems to require prior knowledge.

I could say that it is *evident* to me that a circle is round based on what I have been taught to call its shape and what I can objectively measure in terms of its geometry. But is that self-evidence? Whatever the case, I was coached on what to call it and how to analyze it. It is not self-evidence if I rely on past knowledge to make the connection between circle and roundness. It's simply the pairing of a visual stimulus and a verbal response. This idea can be taken further.

I am familiar with what a circle is and how its geometry works because of what I was taught. It didn't explain itself or originate its meaning in my mind on its own. My familiarity increased over time to the point of recognizing it automatically. I know this is true because there isn't a person on the face of the earth that will raise any objection to the idea that a circle is round. So what we may want to call self-evidence that a circle is round may be nothing more than a worldwide concurrence that we all were taught the same thing regardless of race, religion, nationality, or any other differentiation one would consider grouping humans into.

What if we said that it is self-evident that a wheel is a circle? The characteristic of a wheel that ties it to our notion of circle is its roundness. The human mind recognizes a distinct similarity between the shape of a wheel and the roundness of a circle. Is the self-evidence of a wheel's roundness based solely on its similarity to the shape of a circle? Perhaps this self-evidentiality is secondhand because it depends on the two factors related to a circle, one being its assigned shape name and the other its mathematical argument.

Now what if we said it is self-evident that a wheel rolls? I think here we are on safer ground because we can push the wheel and watch it go. It self-evidences in real time that it rolls. Or is it actually doing that? Its self-evidencing required prompting first. Or maybe, this isn't self-evidencing at all because it did not elicit its own movement within itself. It merely continues to translate the movement imparted to it by the hand of the pusher. So all that possibly could be said about the wheel's motion is that it is self-evident that the wheel was activated by an outside force because you observe it traversing a distance across a span of time. Is it possible that an argument for self-evidence can only be sustained as a result of a prompt? In the case of the wheel, it was set in motion. What set Jefferson in motion? What prompted Jefferson's assertion that all men are created equal?

A wheel rolls because it is round. It is referred to as round because it correlates with the understood shape of a circle. Given this, does a circle itself roll? No. We can safely say that the spoken definition and graphic representation of a circle does not roll. However, a rigid enough object in the shape of a circle will roll if it is acted upon either directly or indirectly by an outside force. Thank you, Mr. Newton!

Now what if during preschool, after the teacher holds up the picture of a circle and tells the children to call the shape "round," he shows a poster of an Asian person and says, "Repeat after me: 'human.'" Moreover, what if she repeated this procedure with every variety, shape, and color of human she could pull together on posters. It seems to me that what's good for calling a circle round is certainly good for calling any person on planet Earth human. Wouldn't such a process teach children learn to pair the outward appearance of any person in the world with the word *human*? And as the child grows, he or she could be taught to more fully value the life of each person and act in the best interest of all people.

To begin the process, the teacher could hold up a poster of a human face and say, "Repeat after me, Asian, human, valuable, worthwhile" or "African, human, valuable, worthwhile" or "Hispanic, human, valuable, worthwhile" or "White, human, valuable, worthwhile." If this was done over the world, there could arise within a generation or so a worldwide recognition and respect for the humanity of every person which could reduce negative considerations of race and bigotry-driven differentiations based on superficialities to complete irrelevance. Even if this suggestion is overly optimistic, a partial realization of it might alter the stubborn bent of humanity on its own destruction.

Is there any hope for the human race? The way we are currently relating to each other on this planet is unsustainable. The countdown clock to our own extinction has already started. Must we ultimately see the blinding flash on the horizon that ends our existence to the dying drone of "Ashes, ashes, all fall down"? Sigh! Sorry.

What if the teacher held up a dozen roses of different varieties and colors and as she pulls them one at a time out of the bunch at random asks, "What is this?" The children respond, "A flower!" Some would say, "A rose." They respond similarly to each one. Here again, the children are taught that the colors of them, the smells of them, and the shapes of them qualify them all as roses of one sort or another.

There is a problem, however, with how human beings relate to each other. Too often, people assign to themselves and others who look like them much greater value and worth than to others who do not. Yes. I'm talking about the P-word, and I realize there are people who take serious umbrage at being labeled as prejudiced. So I'll spin it. That's the American way, isn't it?

From now on, let's refer to them as *selective human phenotype analysts*. How does that sound? When someone asks them what that means, they can say, "We evaluate and pass judgment on the superficial characteristics of others in order to accept or reject them using ourselves as the standard of measurement." The sad thing about this is the average American, on hearing that explanation, would say, "Hmm. Okay. That's interesting," and leave it at that!

> *"We hold these truths to be self-evi-dent, that all men are created equal."*

From the time these words were first written until now, they've been essentially "left at that." Sure, we think quite fondly of ourselves in terms of these words, much like donning a superhero cape with those words embroidered on the back. Evidently, it became quite easy to forget that those words were there as our nation spread westward beyond the Appalachians, taking land from the indigenous Native Americans or making promises to them first, in writing of course, and then later taking even more of their land from them.

Think about it. What if a group of strangers walked uninvited onto your property one day, pitched tents, started digging holes, chopping down your trees, building fences to block your heretofore unlimited right of way, and began erecting homes for themselves. You'd definitely resist such an intrusion, such an invasion by any means at your disposal, even to the extent of armed conflict with the invaders. You would protect your home with every fiber of your being and your countrymen would celebrate your bravery and resolve. Is this how Native American resistance was viewed by those who rehearse the premise of the Declaration? No. They weren't considered noble or righteous in their resistance to the spread of transplanted Europeans across the country-side—their countryside. So—here we are!

"We hold these truths to be self-evi-
dent, that all men are created equal."

Oh, how our hearts are moved as we sing the words, "Oh, beautiful, for taken land!" Oh! I'm sorry? Should I have sang "spacious skies"? Perhaps American skies haven't been that spacious after all because if they were, there may have been enough room for transplanted Europeans and Native Americans to sing together in peace from sea to shining sea. Perhaps spacious skies and enough room are in the eyes of those wielding the biggest stick! "Speak softly and carry a big stick!" Is that it? Sorry, dear late President Roosevelt. Others before you beat you to that punch! Peace through threat! Is that our truth, justice, and American way?

If anything *is* self-evident, it is that in our present-day nuclear-weapon-armed world, all men are equally annihilable? Is this the way nations of the world should posture themselves against each other in order to secure peace? This is not peace! No. It's an international threat-based contest of targeting computers, with batteries definitely included.

> *"We hold these truths to be self-evident..."*

It is both amazing and troubling to me that the United States came into being and struggled to become what it is today based on Jefferson's clever wordsmithery. His words formed the basis of our rallying cry, call to arms, and expenditure of our last full measure of devotion to become a nation. It is amazing to me because he proffered an idea that has no material existence. It's like an ethereal carrot held out and reached for whenever the words, "We hold these truths to be self-evident" are spoken. It's our solemn mantra repeated without thought and believed without evidence.

> *"We hold these truths to be self-evident..."*

These words, on the other hand, are troubling to me because their use in the Declaration of Independence indicts us in our hypocrisy. The country cannot continue to hide behind these words while violating them with impunity on a daily basis. We swell with such pride when they are heard. We speak with such conviction when we say them. I ask, however, what are we doing on a daily basis to actualize them?

> *"We hold these truths to be self-evident..."*

These words remind me of a line from a Robert Frost poem entitled "Mending Wall" that reads, "Good fences make good neighbors." In the poem, Frost describes how he and his neighbor meet at a certain time along their property line to repair and rebuild the stone wall (fence) between them. His neighbor holds the belief that good fences make good neighbors. He doesn't explain it or feel any need to. He just believes in acting on it because it was told to him by his father, and he likes thinking of that saying without venturing beyond it.

> *"We hold these truths to be self-evident, that all men are created equal."*

We love to think of these words from time to time when occasion calls for it. Yet how many of us are willing to go beyond them, to verify them, and bear witness of them in our daily interactions? Well, don't feel bad. I'm sure Mr. Jefferson meant well when he penned those words. Perhaps he did not grapple with philosophical implications of the words in any way similar to how they are being treated in this book.

The stakes were high. Jefferson needed a viable rationale upon which to base the Declaration, a rationale anchored in a liberal view of governance that could be argued effectively against the imposing conservatism of the British crown. So he chose to begin with self-evident equality and endowment with inalienable rights. This would be the basis of the Declaration; its grand *légitime défense.*

Jefferson could have written, "We hold these truths to be valid assumptions." In response, British would certainly have asked, "Why? Why are they valid assumptions?" No. Jefferson already knew that King George wouldn't allow any move on the part of the colonies to separate from the crown. So he chose to base his argument on a plausible turn of words. While it wasn't his original intent, I believe Jefferson's use of the expression "self-evident" became greater than the sum of the original part he intended it to play.

The United States of America is far from being as Christian or religious as it was in Jefferson's day. However, the fact of the mention of the *Creator* in the Declaration that has persisted until today, along with the words "under God" in the Pledge of Allegiance, seems to support at least a de facto belief in the concept of God among Americans. Is it self-evident? Or is it not?

Finally, what if Jefferson had written

> *We hold these truths to be self-evident, that all men are uniquely created and are endowed by their Creator with certain inestimable qualities, principal of which are empathy, charity, and the pursuit of magnanimity.*

But we're not there yet. Sigh!

> *"We hold these truths to be self-evident, that all men are created equal."*

Let's start with this idea. If this is the right platform on which to continue into our national future, we need to stand resolutely on it. If it is not, regardless of how pleasant it sounds, we must redact it from the Declaration, stop giving it lip service, and resign ourselves to being what we actually are.

There is, however, a third alternative. By accentuating equity instead of equality, we may be more successful, as equity or fairness is actionable and reproducible. It is a construct that needs no wrangling to notice and no tedious parsing to comprehend. The results of equity are self-evident in their own right.

How about this?

> *"We hold these truths to be self-evident, that all men are entitled to equity."*

Oh, how I wish Mr. Jefferson had given much more thought to this passage in the Declaration. It is loaded with possibilities. Perhaps if it had been crafted as shown above, he could have claimed an inalienable right to fair treatment, which I believe he sought. Separation from Great Britain would likely have not occurred if equity had been achieved in our relationship with the crown. As it is, however, we drew up our Declaration and carried it resolutely into battle.

Self-evident equality was not defined or achieved by the Revolutionary War, the War of 1812, or the final dissolving of political ties with England. The smoke cleared and the dogs of war stopped barking because, in the end, the British had overextended their supply lines and were unable to continue fighting. Unchecked expansion of an empire always results in reaching a point where reach exceeds grasp. Besides, it didn't make financial sense for them to continue the effort. As a result, the British sailed away and left us here clinging to our self-evident truths. Or did they?

CHAPTER 4

The Premise

The word *premise* means "a statement or idea that is accepted as being true and that is used as the basis of an argument." It is also defined as "an idea or theory on which a statement or action is based." Combining the two definitions, one gets: "A statement, idea, or theory that is accepted as being true and is used as the basis of an argument or action." Logic dictates that if we regress far enough along the continuum of thought, peeling away the many layers upon which our existence is based, we must arrive at an initial founding idea, thought, event, or premise.

For those who believe in the scientific origin or the universe, the big bang theory is the starting premise. They support that premise with observations that indicate that the universe is expanding and that idea thought in reverse must mean that the universe had, at some point, previously contracted to a hot dense state before exploding out to its current ever-expanding extent. Proponents of this idea are quite content to hold on to it, even though they have no idea where the hot dense stuff of the universe actually came from. They call their grasp of the origins of the universe *scientific reason-*

ing. The glaring hole, the how of energy and matter coming to be at a particular point and time in space and ready to explode, is left unexplained.

We seemingly reach an endpoint beyond which human thought and logic is unable to regress. So to say the Big Bang happened, one must, at least involuntarily, take the initial hot dense state as being there just before that grand explosion on faith. Scientists don't want to call it faith at all. That said, there is a limit to our understanding of science. There are even more limits to measuring something that we are an inseparable part of. We cannot currently go beyond our existence in order to know where the stuff that is said to have blown up in the Big Bang came from.

There are those who believe that "in the beginning, God created the heavens and the earth." Either this statement is the most profound premise that mortal minds have ever encountered or it is the most ridiculous assertion ever uttered or written. Choosing to believe in it and rejecting the big bang theory requires the same ingredient (faith in an initial premise) that it takes to embrace the big bang.

Disagree? Okay. Consider the following discussion: The scientific idea of entropy asserts that systems tend to naturally degrade from a state of order to disorder. A simple example is your closet at home. An arrangement of clothing on hangers separated by category such as shirts, pants, sweaters, and coats must be deliberately executed. This execution requires the expenditure of energy as well as a plan or design. If one regresses far enough, previous to the act of putting things away in the closet in an orderly fashion, one must acknowledge that the closet itself was built for that very purpose. Random action cannot account for the specific planning needed to originate and execute a design.

Now follow closely the level of organization of your closet from the point it is first set up so neatly until a month or so later. Without a deliberate effort to maintain the initial state of order established in the closet, the clothing become all mixed up on their hangers—things end up on the floor, hangers are broken or bent down in the middle, and the general appearance of the closet has worsened. Things are never accidentally placed on hangers correctly, buttoned down, and hung neatly by category in one's closet. It's done deliberately at a cost of time, thought, energy, and intentional effort.

The mind-boggling sophistication of the human body, right down to its various cells, so greatly indicates such an infinite level of genius in design and biomechanical/electrical execution as to indicate to me that chance or accidental coming together of this or that to bring about the order and design of us and our world is far above the pay grade of chance events compounding and combining to accomplish the task. So to the creationist, intelligent design suffices as the starting premise for all things bright and beautiful. Now who's right?

I posit that both are. It is possible that a big bang occurred. How do we know, however, if it was one big bang or two or a thousand? I posit that big bangs are constantly going on in the universe. We are such miniscule specks in the grand scheme of things that we can only see and understand what our senses, puny instruments, and limited mental capacities allow us to see and understand. I further posit that the scale upon which we base our observations is so insignificant compared to the immensity of the universe that it is quite possible that the big bang that we assumed started everything may actually be no larger than the explosion of an atomic bomb to an ant with a very gifted imagination. We can't really see this thing because we're inside this thing.

What about the creationists out there? The purposeful design of things, animate and inanimate, more than convinces them of the existence of a *being* that is as advanced beyond us as we are beyond the level of the amoeba. Each camp chooses to embrace a starting premise, and each camp chooses to worship at an altar of faith built at the far limit of their ability to explain all things down to an ultimate theory of everything that makes sense to them.

Consider this: How far out in all directions from the earth does outer space go? Hmm? If, as I have been taught, space extends infinitely in all directions, then the earth must logically be the center of the universe and so is every other imaginable location in space. This must mean that every human being is at the center of the/a universe. How can this be? Perhaps there is more than one way to look at our universe and existence itself.

Is it possible that each person exists in his or her unique perspective universe that is infinite in all directions? What if the perspective universes of all things overlap and share physical, chemical, gravitational, and biological properties in common with each other? If this is the case, then it must be a property of space itself to accommodate this overlap. Because space is infinite, or we believe it to be so, it has no boundaries. And if it has no boundaries, whatever is way out there to us is no closer to the end of the universe than we are here on earth.

It is clear from the foregoing discussion that we need our premises to tame the parameters of our existence into packages that human experience can deal with. The notion of infinitely extending distance in all directions from any given point in space boggles the human brain, perhaps because the brain itself has physical limits in its size and is configured to comprehend existence in terms of boundaries and limits. It would take a boundless mind to comprehend a boundless universe—a mind that is not encased in a cranial cavity, but a mind that consists of a form of energy that originates and permeates all things everywhere. Could the universe be simply a thought?

> *"We hold these truths to be self-evident, that all men are created equal."*

CHAPTER 5

Created Equal

What does *equal* mean? Does it mean that "something consists of the same exact substance as another thing" or that "something can hold the same volume as another identical thing," such as two fifty-gallon steel drums compared to one another?

Are two ice cream cones that have the same amount of ice cream served on them equal? Well, certainly, if the mixture is homogenous, the ice cream will be consistent throughout and dispense quite similarly from the serving machine. If the attendant is careful and exacting, he can quite possibly eyeball quite nearly the same amount of ice cream into each of two cones.

A meticulous ice cream shop worker may try to weigh two empty ice cream cones separately on an analytical scale, pinch off milligrams of extra cone crumbs with fine tweezers from one cone, and reweigh it repeatedly to make it equal in weight to the other. Then, with equal meticulousness, he'd fill the two cones with ice cream and then scrape ultrathin portions of ice cream off the top of one cone or the other to make the two of them balance to the nearest milligram. Now if this were the case, the time spent equalizing those cones would certainly end his employment.

You see, the job of that ice cream shop worker is to make ice cream cones, not equal cones. Any person who grew up eating ice cream cones and watched them being made would likely say that they never gave any thought to whether or not the cone they received was equal or not equal to a fault to the cone made for the customer that came before them, much less for the customers that followed. It is therefore ludicrous for anyone to posit that all ice cream cones are created equal, even in that very shop. The purpose of enjoying them is not in the least bit thwarted as long as each one measures up in general appearance, taste, and size related to its price category.

When it comes to people, they may seem quite the same or equal like the two cones mentioned above, but they are not. While each person is a cone (a human being), by definition, the amount and mixture of the ice cream (quantitative and qualitative potential) of each person differs, and that is not a bad thing. The quantitative and qualitative differences between human beings account for our diversity or flavor. If we were created equal with no evidence of quantitative or qualitative diversity between us, our lives, in my opinion, would be bland and insufferably boring. What if the only flavor available in ice cream was strawberry! Let's look a little closer at quantitative versus qualitative equality.

The word *quantitative* has to do with countable amounts and measures that can be verifiable by others. Two people can be of equal height or equal weight. These are quantifiable measures that can be verified by others. So clearly, no one would attest to a statement that all men or all women are of the same weight and height. A quick glance at any gathering of humans will prove this to be self-evident.

The word *qualitative* in this sense, however, is a bit more difficult to parse. Qualitative human characteristics involve personality, what is regarded as desirable or undesirable, and the valuation and esteem of others.

In the field of mathematics, the equals (=) sign is used to indicate that two numbers or mathematical expressions are of the same value. While there are countless examples where numbers and mathematical expressions are equal, there also are countless examples where they are not. In terms of mathematics, numbers or expressions are either equal to each other or not equal to each other.

It is common to speak of a number as being approximately equal to another, while saying that a woman is approximately pregnant has no meaning whatsoever. Nevertheless, qualitative assessment and approximation has its usefulness. Consider the following example:

We can say that 3.456 is approximately equal to 3.475. This works well with numbers because approximate equality is an accepted concept that helps bridge the gap between quantitative exactness and qualitative interpretation. It doesn't work, however, with nonmathematical situations such as pregnancy or equality.

Jefferson did not say, "All men are created approximately equal." Even though the sentence may sound a bit silly, it is actually more defensible than the absolute approach of declaring all men to be created equal because it leaves a considerable amount of wiggle room for qualifying one's stance in the argument.

Numbers are also rounded to a nearest place value for convenience when performing calculations where the difference between an exact calculation and an approximation is small enough to not compromise the application of an answer for a desired purpose. For instance, while driving, you notice that the mileage to the next city sign reads ninety-seven miles. The passenger riding in the car with you who didn't see the sign may ask, "How far out are we?" You reply, "About one hundred miles." Clearly, one hundred miles is not equal to ninety-seven miles. However, such rounding up of the actual distance from ninety-seven to one hundred conveys a meaning that is more readily grasped and seems more useful than using the exact figure.

When we speak in terms of quantities being about (almost) this or that amount, we are manipulating the meaning of something that has a specific numerical value on its face into what it could be if we ignore the extent it falls short of what we approximately call it. This is always an add-to process and never a take-away-from process. What do I mean?

If it is 2:57 p.m., no one, when asked what time it is, will say, "It was two fifty-five two minutes ago." No, people normally respond, "It's almost three o'clock."

The Founding Fathers witnessed a document that said quite explicitly that "All men *are* created equal." They didn't say that men were approximately equal or nearly equal. Consider the following examples:

1. Two female patients go to the doctor and their blood pressures are taken. Each of them has a blood pressure of 130/85. Numerically, their blood pressures are equal. However, do their blood pressures mean the same thing? Let's say one patient is twenty-one years old and weighs 150 pounds and the other is ten years old and weighs 150 pounds. Now, are these blood pressures equal? The answer is plain. They are equal only in terms of their numerical readings. That's as far as it goes. A blood pressure of 130/85 is within acceptable limits for a twenty-

one-year-old but could be considered problematic for a ten-year-old. Blood pressures, though numerically registering as the same, are quite individual affairs with regard to their meaning and application to the person so measured.

2. Two budding concert pianists compete in the Tchaikovsky international piano competition. They both make it to the finals and each plays a difficult piano concerto. One plays Grieg's Norwegian Concerto and the other plays Rachmaninoff's Second Piano Concerto. The competition judges end in deadlock on deciding a winner between them and elect to present a first prize to each. Does this mean that the two pianists are equal or that they were created equal? I think not. If we place an equal sign between the two of them and look at them in terms of their ability at the keyboard, the sign would have to be changed to an is-not-equal-to sign ($\neq$) because each concerto requires unique keyboard capabilities. Although each pianist executed the skills required in her performance very skillfully, the skill display of each cannot be compared head-to-head, given the fact that they didn't play the same thing for the judges. What got each of them a first prize was that fact that the judges deemed each performance as a first-place effort on its own merits, where those merits went far beyond the handling of keyboard technical difficulties.

Every human being brings his or her potential to the command performance of life. It is up to each person to explore and develop his or her potential to whatever extent life circumstances allow. While people can be thought of as equal in the sense of having potential itself, that potential is qualified on the basis of individual environments and nurturing. It also involves luck regarding the socioeconomic circumstances of one's birth, the nurturing and support one receives, the types of obstacles that are encountered, how one handles those obstacles if they can be handled at all, and the level of motivation possessed by the individual.

If created equal means that all human beings (except for those who are born with physical or mental exceptionalities) come into the world with equal potential, evidence around us every day does not seem to support this.

Undoubtedly, a child born into a very affluent home has a significant but not an absolute advantage over a child born into poverty. What matters is how each child plays the poker game of life from limping in and playing it safe on one end of the scale to going all-in at the other. How a person learns to recognize and deal with the game of life depends heavily on both inside and outside information, where inside information comes from parents and family members, boy or girlfriend, spouse, and friends. Outside information comes from all others with whom interactions occur. There is no guarantee that the person starting with the largest chip stack will have the winning hand in the end. Best hands are often laid down for a bluff. Fate is a capricious dealer. Many an underdog has been saved on the river when percentages argued otherwise.

Finally, consider the case of identical twins. They are the best example I can think of because they seem to be most nearly equally created. It may be self-evident that two children are identical twins. However, is it self-evident that they are *created equal?*

Identical twins arise from the mitotic division of a fertilized ovum that divides to yield two separate diploid (each has its full complement of twenty-three chromosomes) ova that develop into two babies that seem to be exact copies of each other. Is it self-evident then that identical twins are created equal? They look much like each other, sound much like each other, and often dress alike. Nevertheless, does this make them equal to each other?

Twins tend to be as individual in personality, abilities, ambition, and worldview as nontwins. This is because on the genetic level, there are a number of chromosome variations between them that account for physical differences in brain wiring, attitudes, and personality. In addition, these genetic variations explain the differences people can detect in their facial appearance, how their voices sound, the shape of their bodies, and the gestures they make that helps people tell them apart. Placed side-by-side, identical twins are not equal either morphologically or behaviorally. Moreover, the environment the twins grow up in yields different outcomes for each.

Line ten babies up in a hospital nursery ward side-by-side. If available, place babies of different races in the lineup. Make the picture as diverse as possible. Now stand there and think. Is it self-evident that each baby was created (conceived) either equally or with equal merit? The only way this could be so is to limit the application of the term *self-evident merit* or *equality* to the moment of conception when the father's and the mother's gametes meet and combine their genetic information to establish a unique set of instructions to form a new baby. Regardless of race, the process is the same. If Jefferson was calling the joining of gametes to start a new person "self-evident equal creation," he would have been correct because its self-evidence is the obvious fact that *we're here*! Mr. Jefferson, notwithstanding his towering intellect and through no fault of his own, was not referring to this specific example. Even if he were, there remains a big problem.

The isolated fact that all humans are conceived by the joining of gametes adds up to little more than the consequent birth of babies, if they are carried to full-term and delivered. Beyond this, proclaiming that they are endowed by their *creator* with certain inalienable rights is an add-on, an extension, a wish, a manner of thinking arising from moral or religious thinking that imputes regard and value upon all men (people) from the moment of their conception.

Right-to-lifers are of this variety. They are deeply devoted and morally driven to protect the opportunity and potential of all conceived humans. The origin of this position goes something like this: God made Adam and Eve. He endowed them with life, liberty, and the freedom to pursue happiness in the garden of Eden. Once they ate of the forbidden fruit and lost their innocence, they were expelled from the garden. Outside of the garden, they had children. It was up to them to care for their children and endow them, as far as they were able, with love, learning, and protection. They imitated the pattern of watch-care that their *creator* had provided for them. To this day, like-minded like-hearted people do the same thing.

On the other hand, there is the right-to-choose group. They cannot refute biology by denying that conception establishes a complete genetic package which, if given time, will develop into a new unique human being. No. They make what is to them a very straightforward choice to interrupt the development process.

If the right to life was inalienably endowed by the *creator*, wouldn't it be impossible to interrupt the process? Inalienable is as inalienable is enforced. Surely, the *creator* would have built in safeguards against any effort to do so? What if any attempt to bother or interrupt a pregnancy resulted in life-threatening reactions in a woman's body every time? As the *creator* possessed the infinitely complex intellect and insight to build a living human body from the dust of the ground, it would not have been the slightest stretch for him to include fail-safes against any attempt to interrupt a pregnancy in progress. If that was the case, it would be highly unlikely that any abortions would ever be tried, as the whole point of getting an abortion is to cancel an expected baby's birthday so that its mother may go on with her life without the bother—I mean the baby—and not die!

There must be a reason why it isn't this way. Why is there no built-in anti-abortion anaphylaxis? The problem is, if the *creator* had made this so, there would be no option to choose. Consequently, the right to life is not inalienable. It can be denied because babies are aborted every day. What it seems the *creator* made inalienable is the right for humans to choose either of the two options discussed here.

Though this is a troubling and soul-searching decision to face, I believe the *creator* got it right. He allows us to choose the good, the bad, or the ugly for ourselves. It seems that the Supreme Court of the United States of America also got it right by protecting human agency, human free will. It's not a pleasant or happy decision. Beware, however, all will be judged according to their choices.

Do I agree with abortion? No. If the situation arose, would I try to persuade women to have their babies and allow them to be adopted by people who want to love and raise them? Yes! Will I stand in front of an abortion clinic trying to humiliate abortion seekers by hurling scathing imprecations at them? No. Will I use force to try to stop women from having an abortion? No. Will I attempt to rescue any abandoned newborn and get it to safety? Absolutely!

The reason I ventured down this road was an attempt to give fair treatment to each side. Jefferson wrote in the

Declaration about having a "decent respect to the opinions of mankind" regardless of where those opinions or positions arise from. These opinions and positions include for some and exclude for others a belief in God, whatever that means to them.

"All men are created equal." Are they?

CHAPTER 6

—⧓—

Inequality?

When a clothing designer creates a new fashion line, she seeks to produce a variety of looks that are versatile in utility, practical to maintain, and aesthetically appealing. The power and appeal of her clothing line arise from the constructive differences among the looks she offers. No person, other than perhaps Matlock, would enjoy a closet full of the same exact outfit to be worn every single day.

Walk through the produce section of any grocery store. No two potatoes, apples, oranges, pears, peaches, heads of lettuce, yellow squashes, watermelons, bunches of celery, or bananas are equal to each other. If they were, shoppers would not spend so much time picking over them trying to find the ones they want. Every individual item of produce has its own appearance, shape, and nuance of taste, even within the same fruit or vegetable category. In the end, the taste of our cooked food is the algebraic sum of the individual similarities and differences between the food ingredients we combine to make a meal. Think about how boring our meal-times would be if every piece of fruit or vegetable looked and tasted exactly the same within each of their categories. Most people would grow disinterested in eating after a time. Sorry, weight watchers!

No two Remington rifles are created equal, even if they both sport the same model number. They each have idiosyncrasies and inexactitudes, however minute, that give each rifle a custom feel in the hands of its owner. An experienced gun owner who is blindfolded would know the difference between his Remington and that of another person if a switch was made without his knowledge. In addition, consider the rifling characteristics of each Remington. As each bullet traverses its way through and out the end of the barrel, a spin is imparted to it because of a spiral groove that was etched into the inner surface of the barrel. This leaves a unique telltale mark or rifling on each bullet that is as distinctive and reliable as a fingerprint. This is how forensic scientists match certain bullets to certain guns. This is a very valuable and needful example of inequality that allows crimes involving guns to be solved.

The instruments in an orchestra are quite thankfully not created equal. A composer who knows the range, sound, and resonance characteristics of each instrument can combine their sounds thousands of different ways to achieve all of the effects that an orchestra is capable of.

There is nothing more exhilarating than to sit midway back in the second main floor left-of-center section at Carnegie Hall and listen to the New York Philharmonic in full flight as they play the finale of Rachmaninoff's Third Piano Concerto with Vladimir Horowitz at the keyboard. Thank God the orchestra instruments are unequal, unique, and distinct in their characteristics. As Mr. Horowitz accelerates to the finale, the orchestra swells and builds intensity until together the final note is struck. As this happens, sound rebounds off the farthest walls of the concert hall in a shock wave that drives the audience shouting to their feet with thunderous applause! To be immersed in that experience while personally adding to it is quite remarkable. A memorable ovation is a type of performance in and of itself which can never be duplicated. It can be a spontaneous declaration of approval and acceptance on one extreme or just a show of manners on the other.

An artist can tell how well she did in her performance by the signature sound of the applause at the end. It is a sound that does not lie. If she connected deeply with her audience, the applause will have the distinct sound of urgency that often begins before she has played the last note, like a type of early balloting of initial claps that seem to open the floodgates to a deluge of emotion and approbation. If, on the other hand, she didn't, the applause will sound like a drain as the stopper is removed, and there isn't that much water in the sink. It's obligatory, short, and gurgles down and out.

No two paintings are created equal. They are endowed by their creator with the qualities to depict what the artist of each had in mind for creating them. Each human being, if brought to a realization of it, is the artist of his or her own portraiture. Each is endowed with his or her unique set of ability brushes, paints of possibility, solvents of choice, and canvasses of opportunity. Each person must either choose to paint him or herself in or out of masterpiece that is his or her life. Resolve is quite an effective solvent that is able to tame and make agreeable the pigments and paints of opportunity and circumstance that must combine to raise an image of life on that canvass of possibility.

All dogs are not created equal no matter how sincerely their owners may declare themselves to be, if they could. Knowledge about different dog breeds is very common and the abundance of dogs running around free or in association with their human owners provides irrefutable self-evidence of their inequality. Perhaps it is better to say that dogs are diverse from one another rather than generalizing them as unequal.

Now the use of the word *inequality* here is not meant to refer to the extent that each breed is loved or hated by humans. It is their quality of unlikeness in terms of size, coat, temperament, and other observables that is the basis of their vast diversity and charm. That diversity seems to satisfy the various interests and desires of those who wish to own and associate with them.

The air masses that envelop the earth are not equal in temperature, pressure, moisture content, particulates, and gaseous mixture. These factors depend on warming effects of the sun, rates of evaporation and condensation, human activity, and a host of other factors. If there was complete equality in the makeup of our atmosphere, where its temperature, humidity, gaseous mixture, density, and barometric pressure are the same all the way around the globe, the earth would likely have absolutely no weather.

It is differences in air pressure that cause the winds to blow. It is differences in humidity and temperature and atmospheric pressure that allow for dew points, condensation, rain, sleet, snow, hail, and frost. Moreover, a stagnant atmosphere devoid of winds would result in flat, waveless oceans. The inequalities in components and energy dispersals within the atmosphere are quite necessary and essential for the health and supportive effectiveness of earth's atmosphere.

The orbits of the planets and their moons are not circular and equal but elliptical. With respect to the earth's orbit, part of the time, it is closer to the sun; while during another part of the orbit, it is farther away. This arrangement also occurs with the other planets in our solar system and with the moons that orbit those planets, including our own moon. All orbits are not created equal.

Consider the grass that grows in your yard, if you have grass. The blades are not created equal. Each one grows independently in company with the other blades around it. If you get down and look at eye level across the tip of the blades, you will see diversity. Different heights of blades are abundantly evident. Even if you mow your lawn with a very sharp mower blade, while it may appear to the eye as having become level and equal, close examination reveals that there are still innumerable differences in their heights. The mowing only artificially imposes an approximation of equality to the blades. Therefore, it would be ludicrous to say that all the blades of grass in your yard are mown equally. And who really cares anyway, as long as the overall appearance and functionality of the grass satisfies the owner as she sits with a cold glass of lemonade on her shaded deck admiring her finished product.

Consider this: Repeatedly going over your lawn with the lawn mower only edges the blades closer and closer to a maximum length limit, beyond which you reach a point of diminishing returns where no improvement is possible. Moreover, if you keep running the lawn mower over the same ground beyond this point, you risk damaging your lawn.

I once had an across-the-street neighbor who would meticulously cut his never-walked-on-by-anyone lawn. He'd cut it every week, sometimes five days apart. When the job was done, the lawn looked like one continuous green Mohawk haircut. It was so weird to look at. It seemed to me that he paid a very high price for his attempt to create absolutely equal grass.

Here's the connection. Successive rulings of the Supreme Court in civil rights cases have not established that "all men are created equal." While the court decided against segregationist practices associated with school attendance, public transportation, voting rights, and housing options, to name a few, it is the avoidance of penalties for noncompliance that has brought about social change. I was not privy to the deliberations of the supreme court justices as they considered the constitutional merits of the civil rights cases before them. However, I am quite certain that the court reached its decisions based on how the constitution reads rather than on any premise of created equality. While there is no mention of created equality in the constitution, the words "all men are created equal" likely had a practical effect on the thinking of the court.

I don't think that human equality can be realized. If by *equality* we mean "equal access to the ways and means of prosperity," this will never occur because access varies from person to person for reasons within and outside of their control. Besides, efforts put forth by governments to artificially impose such equality ultimately fail.

What about income equality. Well, this will never happen in America. There is no motivation or practical path for achieving it. Politicians bring up the subject during elections to garner votes from those whose incomes are lacking compared to those whose incomes are abundant, as if whole socioeconomic groups can be elevated to parity with those above them in income on the updraft of a politician's soaring speeches.

Admittedly, there are people who earn the same amount of money on an hourly or salary basis because they enter a particular job title at the same time. For instance, all teachers in a given school system who have the same degree and years on the job level earn the same salary. I'm not talking about this type of categorical salary sameness. No. I'm talking about the liberal mumbo jumbo dished out to eager audiences that sounds like promises to "fix it" so that regardless of life circumstances and personal decisions, somehow the economic lower-downs will miraculously make more so that their income will rise to a level equal to those of higher education and career attainments.

The idea of people being created equal does not guarantee that they experience equal opportunity. No two opportunities are equal or the same. They may be similar in many respects, but they are never the same.

Created equality may include the assumption that two individuals possess identical genotypic and phenotypic characteristics. This situation does not exist in nature. *Opportunity*, on the other hand, is "a set of circumstances that makes it possible to do something." We have already established that no two human beings arrive on planet earth as equals, even at birth. Moreover, the circumstances that make it possible for each of them to do a particular thing operate independently as seen from the point of view of each of their life experiences. The obverse side of this coin is the door or pathway through which each individual desires to pass.

The requirements for passing through such doors are controlled by the doorkeepers. For example, the requirements for getting into a particular college may include achieving a certain score on the ACT test. Two individuals pay their testing fees and show up at testing center on the same day and are admitted. From the standpoint of the testing service, each of them has been afforded an opportunity to take the test. That's only half of the ticket. Their individual preparation for the test is the key circumstance that makes it possible for them to do well or not, to the extent that their life experiences have facilitated sufficient preparation.

Life experiences vary, and there are a number of factors within the control or beyond the control of each person that add to or significantly subtract from the preparation lead-ing up to the moment of the test. Where you are born, the economic status of your family, the education level of your parents, the challenges and barriers you encounter, the deci-sions you make along the way, your level of motivation, the encouragement and guidance that you either receive or do not receive, the quality of your educational experiences, and a host of other factors either buoy you up or sink you under during your journey. This half of the ticket is yours to make of it what you can.

A big problem arises when, in the name of equal oppor-tunity, the doorkeepers make exceptions to allow the admit-tance of those who would otherwise be unqualified. If con-siderations of race, sexual orientation, and religion that have been addressed by the supreme court are respected on the basis of equity or fairness, hopefully what remains are the equitably applied requirements for walking through what-ever door of opportunity one encounters. Here, too, these remaining requirements must not exploit the socioeconomic disadvantages of certain groups in order to deliberately exclude them from successful entry. Ideally, such selection processes should be impartial and unbiased. For this very rea-son, quota schemes are inherently discriminatory. If so, what are we left with?

It seems to me that the most effective way to improve the chances of the disadvantaged is to first encourage and support nuclear families and other parenting partnerships that are able to reproduce similar positive results. Next, suffi-cient social and economic scaffolding is needed to maximize the preparation of the disadvantaged to respond to the oppor-tunities that may arise in life. And what is this scaffolding? It starts with strong early education programs that compensate for the lack of exposure to ideas, images, sounds, objects, and language that would leave such students at a severe disadvantage going forward. After this, the emphasis of education must be to inspire inquiry on the part of the student rather than coaching them to pass standardized tests. Our current public education system guarantees continued racial disparities in student achievement and educational outcomes.

There was a period of time several decades ago when achievement gaps between say black and white students essentially disappeared. During those years, funding for early childhood education, when language development and mental models that enrich subsequent learning are most effective, was strong and persistent. Within a few years after, Head Start and other early intervention funding was cut; the disparities reemerged and have grown ever wider.

Robert Frost in the poem "Mending Wall," where the two neighbors repair the stone wall between them, characterized their activity by saying what they were doing was "just another kind of outdoor game—one on a side. It comes to little more." It seems that too many of our citizen-to-citizen interpersonal relationships are like that game. Everyone has internalized the script and plays along instinctively—with each person, racial identity group, religion, and political persuasion dutifully coloring within the lines of his or her decided positions while chafing inwardly when confronted by those who dare to create and "color" their own book of experience drawing from the palette of acceptance.

Good fences only pretend to make good neighbors. They define the limit between where someone's "whatever" stops and someone else's "whatever" begins. They are a standing testament of division that both defines and defies. Fences segregate. They limit in what we can do behind them and limit out much of the good that could be done for us. If left unchallenged, they maroon us in a place of circular argument over the righteousness of our rightness.

Imagine an America where striving for equality has become immaterial, where every effort to be the best "whatever" one can be is encouraged and accepted. The way forward is more likely along the path of equity rather than equality.

I hold this truth to be inalienable, that all people must be treated equitably.

CHAPTER 7

Equity

The Founding Fathers said, "We hold these truths to be self-evident, that all men are created equal."

Perhaps it would have been far more benevolent, useful, helpful, and meaningful for Jefferson to have written, "We take the position that all men possess value and are entitled to fair treatment [equity]." If he had done this and declared to King George that they are willing to go to war in protest against England's treatment of them, the whole argument about equality and inalienable rights could have become major intrinsic philosophical components of their intent rather than the launching pad of their rebellion. Lots of times, more of what you want to get out there can get out there when you're more particular about how much of what you put out there in the first place.

People are absolutely not equal to each other. They do, however, have value in themselves and can choose to recognize, associate with, employ, celebrate, utilize, partner with, leverage, respect, and love the value in others. The push for human equality has sought to achieve this very state but with very limited success because, in reality, it wasn't a matter of the equality of men but the equity of men.

Human life is devalued in a wholesale way in the entertainment industry. We depict violence of every horrible type and hideous variety. Millions sit and watch every imaginable way someone can be made to suffer, bleed, beaten, cut, shot, incinerated, and blown to bits. We create video games that glorify those who have no regard for human life. Watch any superhero movie, and for a change, count the number of people who are killed by the good guys or girls. You would be surprised at the total count by the end of the movie. We give the so-called good guys a psychological pass on their infliction of violence on people we are hypnotized into believing that they should die or deserve to die. The cost of this experience is that it eviscerates us and reduces us to empty shells. It eats at our personal equity (value) while conditioning us to overlook or flagrantly ignore the value of others.

After the show ends, it doesn't actually end. In the back of the mind of the viewer, the show continues on a subconscious level influencing attitudes and behaviors. Many people act out the violence they have witnessed. It may not be on the spectacularly bloody and hideous level shown on TV or at the movies with all of the sound and special effects, but it happens when old people are attacked by the young who videotape themselves sucker punching one of them. It happens when robbers shoot an unsuspecting convenience store owner over a couple of dollars. It happens when a husband punches his wife or a boyfriend hits his girlfriend. It happens on the playground when elementary children poke each other with a sharpened pencil or a high school student takes out a concealed automatic weapon and kills students and several teachers.

When we look at each other, we should see value and worth coming into our eyes and hearts. But unfortunately, when we look at each other, too often we see nothing and acknowledge nothing.

Jefferson said, "We hold these truths to be self-evident, that all men are created equal."

Given the foregoing discussion, I say, "I hold this truth to be self-evident, that all men, women, boys, and girls are created with an initial endowment of human quality and potential that can increase through equitable treatment of themselves by others and of others by themselves."

Equity or fairness is both definable and defensible. In addition, unlike the notion of equality, it is detectable and demonstrable. Finally, what makes equity most effective is that it is actionable. It can be applied from person to person, regardless of outward appearance, as long as there is mutual acceptance between parties about just what is fair.

It seems quite interesting to me at this point that this whole discussion has boiled down to a restatement of the golden rule. Doing unto others as you would have them (not "before they") do unto you seems to sum this up quite nicely. I didn't plan to end on this note, but it seems to fit perfectly.

Finally, there have been so many times that as I walked along in a store, I would encounter a person walking in the opposite direction. We would make eye contact, and without saying a single word and without breaking our stride, we would give each other a little nod as we passed. In that brief moment, we were connected humanity. In that brief moment, we validated each other's quality and worth. During that brief encounter, we lifted each other through an offered and accepted exchange and acknowledgment of the other's worth. We never stopped to become introduced, to learn each other's name, or to become fast friends. There was no need for that. What we did strengthened the fabric of our shared humanity through an accepting glance. Then we went on, buoyed by the silent wordless lift we received from each other. At least, for my part, I did. How could we relate if we didn't see each other?

Do we hold these truths to be self-evident?

CONCLUSION

I am fully aware that daring to question the premise used by the founders to declare independence from Great Britain could start a fire that creates its own weather and sustains itself with twists and turns of righteous indignation and abundant self-evident oxygen!

"We hold these truths to be self-evident, that all men are created equal."

We've said it enough times. We've prayed it enough times. We've preached it in our pulpits and sung it in our choirs. We've taught it in our schools. We've marched buoyed by it into war and died for it in our battles. Many have given the last measure of their blood for it. In perpetuity for all to see, we've erected granite monoliths, columned memorials, and monuments to immortalize it.

I am fully aware that my questioning of the premise will never unearth it. Its roots run far too deep into the groundswell of our national enthusiasm for being. We've literally deified it. "Praise its righteous intent!" It lives and breathes through the circular mantra: *Est per se notum est, quia illud est per se notum est.* "It is self-evident because—it is self-evident."

Ahhhummmmmmmmmmmmmmmm!

If created equality is self-evident, then self-evidence is created equality. Is this true? This notion seems to meet the bar of a fallacy that affirms the consequent. Take heart, reader.

I think, in conclusion, that the premise *can* work in a limited sense if it is carefully parsed and qualified. We'll talk about that later. However, the problem continues to be that the premise is not generally evinced on the stage of our everyday human experience.

The premise of equal creation is deeply ingrained. I'll accept it, for now, because of its power to inspire. However, for practical purposes, we need a premise of "justice and equity" to underpin our daily dealings with each other and our shared planet. This alternate premise is not ethereal. Its sustenance is not sentimental self-evidence. It must emerge day-to-day from cooperation between people that can generate a protective pragmatic field over our planet to stave off hatred and, perhaps, postpone mankind's insane propensity for self-destruction! However, such a détente is not sustainable. Love has something to do with it.

"And that's the way it is." Isn't it?

ABOUT THE AUTHOR

The author is a retired educator and private school principal who resides in Greenville, Mississippi. He is originally from Nebraska, where he acquired strong Midwestern values of hard work, honesty, and acceptance of others. His worldview is that of a pragmatic realist devoted to inviting others into an ever widening circle of inclusion and acceptance.